This is
My Home

Angela Royston

raintree
a Capstone company — publishers for children

Raintree is an imprint of Capstone Global Library Limited, a company incorporated in England and Wales
having its registered office at 264 Banbury Road, Oxford, OX2 7DY – Registered company number:
6695582

www.raintree.co.uk
myorders@raintree.co.uk

Edited by Clare Lewis
Designed by Cynthia Della-Rovere
Picture research by Morgan Walters
Production by Laura Manthe
Originated by Capstone Global Library
Printed and bound in India

ISBN 978 1 4747 6215 1
22 21 20 19 18
10 9 8 7 6 5 4 3 2 1

British Library Cataloguing in Publication Data

A full catalogue record for this book is available from the British Library.

Acknowledgements

We would like to thank the following for permission to reproduce photographs: Getty Images: Tim Graham,
7; Shutterstock: Alastair Wallace, 12, Amy Cora Megan, 13, Ana Candida, 5 (top), David Hughes, 15
(top), David Muscroft, 24 (bottom), David Young, 21, DrimaFilm, 14, elleon, 1, Ewelina Wachala, cover
(top), 10, Giancarlo Liguori, 29 (right), Helen Hotson, 20, Jacek Wojnarowski, cover (bottom left), 17,
jamesdavidphoto, 5 (bottom), Karkas, 11, Meirion Matthias, cover (bottom middle), Mr Pics, 15 (bottom),
mubus7, 24 (top), Nodari, 29 (left), Paolo Paradiso, 4 (right), Philip Openshaw, 25, PhotoFires, cover
(bottom right), Richard Hayman, 4 (left), travellight, 28, Tupungato, 16, WDG Photo, 6
Design Elements: Shutterstock

Many thanks to Amal, Poppy, Boadicea and Deron and their families for supplying the photographs of their
homes in this book.

Contents

Some words appear in this book in bold, **like this.** You can find out what they mean by looking in the glossary.

What is a home?

Your home is where you live with your family. It is where you eat, play, sleep and keep yourself clean. There are millions of homes all over the United Kingdom. All homes are different.

Homes can be built of stone, bricks or concrete. Some homes are in the **countryside** and some are in cities. Some homes are by the sea. Some can even move from place to place! Which of these photographs looks most like your home?

Detached houses

A house that stands on its own is called a detached house. Detached houses often have a garden that goes all around the house. There may be room for a climbing frame in the garden. Or it might have a lawn with trees, flowers and a vegetable patch.

Detached houses can be large or small.

This bungalow has a large driveway.

Bungalows are houses with no stairs. All the rooms are on one level. Bungalows are often detached. Detached houses and bungalows often have **driveways** and **garages**.

Amal's detached home

My name is Amal. I live in a detached house in a small town. Even though my house is small, I think it is really cosy. Our road is a **cul-de-sac**. We know all our **neighbours**. Everyone is friendly.

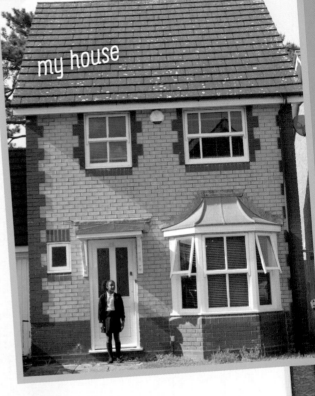

my house

I meet my friends and walk to school. My brothers and I sometimes play football or go rollerblading in the street.

my bed

I share my bedroom with my brother. We have got bunk beds. It's fun to have someone to chat to at night.

the conservatory

Our garden has a huge trampoline. It nearly fills up the whole garden! We have got a conservatory. It's like an extra glass room at the back of the house. Sometimes I do my homework in there.

doing homework

Semi-detached houses

A semi-detached house shares one side wall with another house. The two houses sometimes look like mirror images of each other. Their gardens are usually separated by a fence or a wall.

One of these semi-detached houses is higher than the other.

The people living in this house like bright colours!

Although semi-detached houses often look the same on the outside, they may be very different inside. People like to **decorate** in different ways. Some people like bright colours and patterns. Some people like pale or dark colours.

All in a row

A terraced house is attached to other houses on both sides. Some terraced houses have narrow gardens at the back. Many terraced houses have **yards** at the back. People sometimes hang washing or keep bins in their yards.

Houses with chimney pots were built when people had open fires.

These terraced houses have attic bedrooms.

Large terraced houses can be several **storeys** tall. The kitchen and sitting room are usually downstairs and the bedrooms are upstairs. Some houses have a **basement**. This is a floor that is partly below ground. **Attic** rooms are high up, under the sloping roof. Some of the walls slope too!

City flats

In large towns and cities, people live close together. Large buildings are often divided into flats. Different families and groups of people live in them. People can live above and below each other, as well as next door.

These flats may once have been big houses. They have been divided up into flats.

This block of flats has a shared garden.

An **estate** is a collection of several blocks of flats. Most estates have open areas, which everyone shares. Many flats have **balconies**, where people can grow plants in pots.

A balcony provides a bit of outdoor space.

The high life

Some flats are in tower blocks. They are very tall buildings. Tower blocks have lots of flats on top of each other. They have lifts as well as stairs. The lifts carry people up and down to each floor.

This colourful tower block has pot plants on the roof.

These tower blocks each have 15 **storeys.**

Some tower blocks have gardens on the roof! Some even have walkways between them. People who live high up can see far across the city.

17

Boadicea's city home

My name is Boadicea.
I live in a flat in a big city with my mum,
dad and twin brothers, Spike and Jago.
I share a bedroom with my brothers. My
dad built me a platform for my bed. It is
my own special place.

my bed

Our flat is part of an **estate** with lots of flats like ours all around. There are great paths around the estate. They are perfect for riding scooters and bikes on.

We have lots of parks nearby. I like to play on the swings near my home. My school is close by. We walk through the busy streets to get there.

at the park

my garden

Our flat is on the ground floor. I like to play in the garden after school.

Surrounded by countryside

People who live in the **countryside** often live in villages or small towns. Some houses are far away from others. Cottages are small houses. Some cottages have **thatched roofs,** made of straw.

Country cottages can be by the seaside.

Some homes are far from other homes.

Some people live on farms. Their homes are **surrounded** by fields. People in the countryside might have to travel a long way to get to the shops or to visit friends.

Glossary

attic space or rooms in the roof

balcony open platform on the outside of a building above the ground floor

basement lowest floor, built partly below ground level

countryside fields, woods or moors – most of the land outside cities and towns

cul-de-sac road that has no way through; it has a dead end

decorate make beautiful by painting or adding decorations

driveway wide path in front of a building

eco home home that is designed to stay warm or cool without heating or air conditioning

environment all the things together that surround living things in the natural world

estate several blocks of flats or rows of houses built in the same area

lock short section of a canal with gates at each end. The gates can be opened or closed to change the water level, used for raising and lowering boats.

neighbour person who lives nearby

solar panel device that uses the energy of sunlight to make electricity

storey floor of a building

surrounded have something all around

thatched roof covering made with bunches of straw or reeds

yard small, enclosed paved area at the back of a house

Find out more

Books

Children Like Us Homes Around the World, Moira Butterfield (Wayland, 2016)

Homes Around the World, Clare Lewis (Raintree, 2015)

Let's Build a House: A book about buildings and materials, Mick Manning and Brita Granström (Franklyn Watts, 2014)

Website

www.bbc.co.uk/scotland/education/wwww/homes/kids/
A fun website that gets you thinking and experimenting about how you build a home. Click on the What and When buttons.

Places to visit

There are historic homes and museums all over Britain that show you how people lived in the past. Search for "museum of homes and houses" for your area. Here are a few:

www.nts.org.uk/Visit/Tenement-House/ gives you information about a Glasgow tenement museum from 100 years ago.

museum.wales/stfagans/ is in Cardiff and gives details of homes and houses since ancient times.

www.nimc.co.uk/schools-and-learning/programme/150/houses-and-homes/ The Mid-Antrim Museum focuses on houses and homes in Ballymena in the 1920s and the present.

www.wealddown.co.uk/explore/buildings/
The Weald & Downland Living Museum is near Chichester in Sussex. It includes rebuildings of homes and farms over the centuries up to the present day. You can explore them too online.

Index